THE
OZONE LAYER

BY
JANE DUDEN

CRESTWOOD HOUSE
New York
Collier Macmillan Canada
Toronto

Maxwell Macmillan International Publishing Group
New York Oxford Singapore Sydney

Library of Congress Cataloging-in-Publication Data
Duden, Jane.
 The ozone layer / by Jane Duden. — 1st ed.
   p. cm. — (Earth alert)
 Includes bibliographical references.
 Summary: Describes the ozone layer and its important function in protecting the earth from dangerous ultraviolet rays. Also examines the threats posed to the ozone layer by chlorofluorocarbons and other pollutants and what can be done to stop further damage.
   1. Chlorofluorocarbons—Environmental aspects—Juvenile literature. 2. Ozone layer depletion—Environmental aspects—Juvenile literature. [1. Chlorofluorocarbons—Environmental aspects. 2. Ozone layer depletion—Environmental aspects.] I. Title. II. Series.
 TD887.C47D84   1990   363.73'92—dc20   90-36297   CIP
 ISBN 0-89686-546-0   AC

Photo Credits
Cover: Animals Animals: (M. A. Chappell)
Earth Scenes: (Doug Allan) 4; (James David Brandt) 25; (E. R. Degginger) 33
Devaney Stock Photos: (Gunter Marx) 7, 9; (P. Grant) 12, 23
Journalism Services: (Jane M. Aitken) 15
Greenpeace: (R. Visser) 17
NASA: 20
AP—Wide World Photos: 28
DRK Photo: (John and Pat Valenti) 31
Superstock: 36

Copyright © 1990 Crestwood House, Macmillan Publishing Company

Macmillan Publishing Company
866 Third Avenue
New York, NY 10022

Collier Macmillan Canada, Inc.
1200 Eglinton Avenue East
Suite 200
Don Mills, Ontario M3C 3N1

CRESTWOOD HOUSE
Produced by Flying Fish Studio Incorporated

Printed in the United States of America

First Edition

10 9 8 7 6 5 4 3 2 1

CONTENTS

AN URGENT MISSION

The time is noon, but the sky is dark. This is the Antarctic winter—August 1986. At the South Pole, the seasons are just the opposite of ours. The temperature is a bone-chilling 48 degrees below zero. A ski plane lands on the ice. Out of the plane climbs a group of scientists, bundled in bright red parkas. They have arrived at McMurdo Base. McMurdo is the United States headquarters for research at the South Pole.

The scientists are in the National Ozone Expedition—called NOZE for short. Their mission is to search for clues about a hole in the sky over the South Pole. The hole was discovered in 1985. It is a hole in the earth's ozone layer.

The air above the earth is made up of many layers. The ozone layer is 8 to 30 miles above the earth. It acts as a shield for the earth, keeping away some of the sun's rays. While some of the sun's rays warm and give life to the earth, others are dangerous. Ozone keeps

An icy bay in the South Pole, where scientists discovered a hole in the ozone layer.

most of the dangerous rays from reaching us on the ground.

Scientists have many questions to answer. Will the ozone hole occur only over the South Pole? Will it spread to other parts of the earth, where people live? What causes the hole?

The mission is urgent. A breakdown of the ozone layer would mean a threat to all life on earth. Dr. Robert Watson, a space research scientist, sums up the danger: "We must protect the ozone layer or prepare to do a slow burn."

WHAT IS THE OZONE LAYER?
What Is Ozone?

Ozone is a type of natural gas. It is a special form of oxygen. The oxygen we breathe is called O_2. That means two atoms of oxygen form a molecule. You can't see or smell O_2, but it is in the air all around us. We need to breathe oxygen to live.

Ozone is called O_3. That means three atoms of oxygen form a molecule. Ozone is pale blue in color. If there is enough of it in the air, you can see it. But you really do not want to see ozone. Breathing even small amounts of ozone is poisonous to human beings.

Ozone in the air we breathe is dangerous. Ozone that is ten miles above the earth is another story. We need that high, faraway ozone to protect us. At a safe distance, ozone blocks the sun's dangerous ultraviolet rays.

The ozone layer protects all life on earth from the sun's harmful ultraviolet rays.

Where Does Ozone Come from?

Think of the earth as a round ball wrapped in blankets. Each blanket is different. Each is made of different material, and each is a different thickness. Each has a special scientific name.

The first blanket is called the troposphere. This lowest layer is about eight miles thick. This is the air we breathe. Regular oxygen makes up about one-fifth of the air around us. All life on earth exists in this layer.

The second blanket is called the stratosphere. This layer is 8 to 30 miles above the earth. Some of the regular oxygen drifts up into this layer. Ultraviolet rays from the sun hit the oxygen in this layer. The oxygen then breaks up and comes together again to form ozone. That is how the sun makes ozone in the stratosphere.

Ozone close to the ground is made in a different way. It comes from man-made gases and chemicals.

The ozone layer is the ozone high above the earth. There is not much ozone there. If you counted all the gases in the atmosphere, you would find only one particle of ozone in every million. This is still enough. This small amount of ozone protects us from ultraviolet rays. It is enough to absorb most of the ultraviolet rays and keep them from reaching the earth.

Smog hangs in the air over Los Angeles. Too much ozone close to the earth—caused mainly by car exhaust fumes—makes the air unhealthy to breathe.

GOOD OZONE, BAD OZONE

The ozone high above the earth is "good" ozone. It protects us from the ultraviolet rays of the sun. But ozone closer to the earth's surface is "bad" ozone. It causes many serious problems.

If you live in a city, you may have heard about ozone alerts. The alerts tell people when ozone is making the air dangerous to breathe. Too much ozone close to the ground also causes smog.

Ozone at ground level is made when the sun "cooks" certain gases. These gases come from gas tanks, gas stations, car exhaust fumes, and paint fumes. Large cities have more of this dangerous, bad ozone because they have more cars and trucks and industry. Winds can also carry this ozone far from the places where it is made.

A kind of air pollution, this ozone damages crops and forests, costing billions of dollars. What is more, it can irritate people's eyes and skin and permanently damage lungs. The American Lung Association says children are more sensitive to bad air, so ozone pollution can hurt them more than adults. The bodies of children are not ready to deal with the pollution. They also spend more time outdoors, especially in hot weather, when pollution is at its worst. And because children are more active than adults, they breathe in more pollution.

Does that mean that children should always stay indoors? Or that they should never run and jump and play? Of course not! But on days when the air is bad, they need to be careful. That is why the air in cities is measured often.

Air pollution is measured on two different scales. One is the Air Quality Index, or AQI. The other is the Pollutant Standards

Index, or PSI. They are used in different parts of the country. The numbers in each index tell how bad the air pollution is each day. They warn people to slow down or to stay indoors. Here is a PSI chart:

Value (ozone level)	Description	
0 - 50	Good	
50 - 100	Moderate	
100 - 200	Unhealthful	Health advisory
200 - 300	Very unhealthful	Alert
300 - 400	Very unhealthful	Warning
400 - 500	Hazardous	Emergency

When the ozone gets to a PSI of 200, it is time to be careful. Then children are advised not to run or do other exercise outside that makes them breathe hard. When the PSI reaches 235, both children and adults with breathing problems should stay indoors most of the time. All outdoor sports and games should stop.

Ozone levels in many cities have come down in recent years. Laws have cut down on the amount of many kinds of pollution in the air. But there are still high ozone levels in many U.S. cities.

WHY SHOULD WE CARE ABOUT THE OZONE LAYER?

Ozone Protection

The ozone layer developed millions of years ago. Without it, life on earth could not have begun. Before the ozone layer, ultraviolet rays killed any chance of life on earth.

But now humans are destroying the ozone layer. We make chemicals that drift 5, 10, or 15 miles above the earth, where they destroy the ozone. As the ozone layer thins out, more ultraviolet rays reach the earth. All living things may be affected.

Ozone loss is greatest at the South Pole. But the ozone all around the globe is getting thinner. What will happen if this sunscreen keeps getting thinner?

Dangerous Ultraviolet Rays

How much ozone can we afford to lose? Scientists say that losing just 1 or 2 percent will expose us to more ultraviolet rays, which can cause the following dangers:

Skin cancer. Doctors and scientists warn us not to sunbathe. They say that lying in the sun to get a tan can cause skin cancer. Loss of ozone makes this even more dangerous. Ultraviolet rays cause sunburn. One kind of ultraviolet ray is the cause of most skin cancer. This kind is called ultraviolet-B.

Experts say that each percent of ozone we lose will mean more occurrences of skin cancer. A 1 percent loss of ozone might mean

As the ozone layer thins out, people are more exposed to the dangers of sunburn and skin cancer. Doctors now advise everyone to use sunscreens. 13

3 to 6 percent more cases of skin cancer. In the United States, that could mean 43,000 more cases of skin cancer a year.

Skin cancer takes time to develop. We might not see the increase for 30 or 40 years. Doctors warn that we should start protecting ourselves now. They advise anyone playing outdoors to wear sunscreen. They also say to check sunscreen labels for ratings. A sunscreen of at least 15 is best. Experts also advise staying out of the sun from 10 A.M. to 2 or 3 P.M. That is when ultraviolet rays are the strongest.

Damaged immune systems. Ultraviolet-B also weakens the cells in the body that fight cancers and viruses. It therefore lowers the body's defense against disease, making it easier to get sick. The body is less able to fight back. Doctors say that even sunscreens do not protect against this problem.

Blindness. Ultraviolet light also causes cataracts. Cataracts cloud the lens of the eye. They impair vision and sometimes even lead to blindness. More than 600,000 people have cataract operations each year in the United States. More ultraviolet rays would mean more cataracts and more cases of blindness.

Threat to ocean life. Plankton are tiny ocean plants and animals so small you need a microscope to see them. They live in the upper few feet of the ocean, where they use sunlight to make food for fish and almost every other living thing in the water. In fact, without plankton there would be no life in the ocean. But plankton can be hurt by ultraviolet light. The entire food chain of the ocean could collapse. Fish could no longer feed on plankton, and we would no longer feed on fish.

Decreased food supply. Even a slight increase in ultraviolet light can hurt plants and damage crops. Farmers would harvest

One result of a shrinking ozone layer is damaged crops, burned by the ultraviolet rays of the sun.

less corn or rice or wheat or beans. Crop loss means more hunger in the world.

As you can see, the effects of ultraviolet rays are very serious. That's why experts have raced to find the cause of the ozone hole at the South Pole. They agree that we need to protect and restore the "good" ozone layer high above the earth.

AN INVENTION TOO GOOD TO BE TRUE
The Invention of CFCs

Trouble in the ozone layer began in the late 1920s. That is when an American scientist invented a new group of gases. Thomas Midgley, Jr., invented CFCs. Their full name is chloro-fluorocarbons. CFCs are made of three kinds of atoms: chlorine, fluorine, and carbon.

At that time, dangerous chemicals were used to cool refrigerators. Midgley thought his new gases were very safe. He even showed how safe they were by inhaling a deep breath of CFC and then blowing out a candle. At first CFCs did seem harmless. They

Dangerous CFC gases—which destroy the ozone layer—are released when trash is burned or left out in the open to decompose.

were not toxic. They did not break down easily. They did not react easily with other substances. They were good insulators. CFCs were also good coolants. They were simple and cheap to make.

Companies began looking for new ways to use CFCs. Soon, hundreds of millions of pounds of CFCs were made each year. One CFC called freon was used in cooling fluids in refrigerators and air conditioners. Other CFCs were used to make bubbles in plastic-foam cartons. Some were used in foam insulation for homes. Some were used in pillows. Some were used in spray cans for everything from deodorant to bug spray. Some were used to clean electronic parts. CFCs were so useful they seemed too good to be true.

CFCs *were* too good to be true. A chemist at the University of California began to study them. He knew that CFCs lasted a very long time. So he began asking questions: Where were CFCs going? What were they doing to the atmosphere? Did they act the same in the upper atmosphere as they did near the earth? F. Sherwood Rowland made a frightening discovery. When CFCs reach the stratosphere, they attack ozone. They break down the ozone layer. "The work is going well," the worried scientist told his wife. "But it looks like the end of the world."

The Trouble with CFCs

CFC gas escapes when certain items are made or destroyed. For example, when someone throws out an old air conditioner, the air conditioner may go to a town dump. There it is crushed by a bulldozer, which forces CFC gas into the air. Plastic-foam egg cartons are another example. When they are crushed or burned, CFC gas goes into the air. Car air conditioners that leak also release CFCs into the air. According to the Natural Resources Defense Council (NRDC), leaky car air conditioners are the largest source of CFCs in the United States.

After they escape, CFCs drift up to the stratosphere. There they meet the ozone layer. The sun's ultraviolet rays shatter the CFCs, freeing chlorine. Chlorine atoms act like high-altitude Pac-Men, "eating" the ozone. The chlorine stays in the stratosphere for up to one hundred years. Just one chlorine atom can eat as many as 100,000 molecules of ozone.

CFCs and the Greenhouse Effect

CFCs are part of what many scientists believe is another threat to the earth. Along with other gases, CFCs help to warm the earth. One name for this warming is the "greenhouse effect." It is also called global warming.

The earth's lower blanket of gases has always helped to keep it warm. Certain gases help to trap the sun's heat near the earth. This natural heat keeps the earth from being cold and lifeless. But now, more and more "greenhouse gases" are being made in the laboratory. These extra, man-made gases act like the glass in a greenhouse, which traps the heat of the sun. But they trap too much of the sun's heat near the earth.

Like the ozone problem, the greenhouse effect will take a long time to be felt. By the time we feel the warmer temperatures, the damage will have been done. Many scientists think that global warming has already begun.

About half of the total greenhouse effect is caused by carbon dioxide. It comes from burning fossil fuels — coal, gas, and oil. These fuels are burned in power plants, factories, and cars. Other

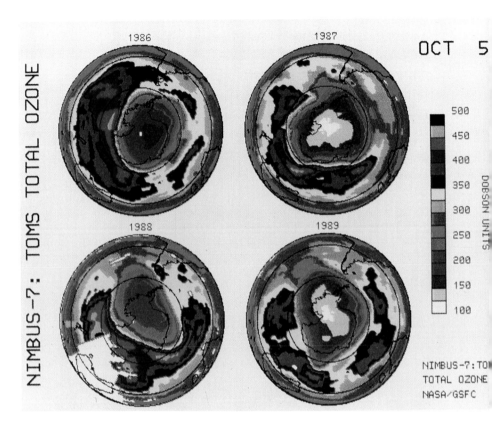

These satellite photos show how the hole in the ozone layer has gotten larger over the past few years.

greenhouse gases are ozone, smog, methane, nitrous oxide, CFCs, and halons. There is much more carbon dioxide in the air than CFCs. But CFCs are 20,000 times more efficient at trapping heat than carbon dioxide. Therefore, getting rid of CFCs would help slow global warming.

WARNING SIGNS
An Early Warning

In 1974, scientists began to warn the world that chlorine in CFCs would destroy the ozone layer. Scientists knew it would take 10 to 15 years for CFCs to reach the stratosphere. Wouldn't it be smart to ban CFCs before they could attack the ozone layer?

To the scientists, the solution was simple. Stop putting CFCs into the air. But companies were making millions of dollars on the sprays, coolants, and plastic containers made of CFCs. They were not willing to give them up so easily. Then scientists proved how dangerous CFCs in spray cans were, and some people listened. They raised a warning cry, "Ban the can!" In 1978, they won a victory. Most CFC use in aerosol spray cans was banned in the United States.

Many people still believed the ozone problem was only a "scare" issue, however. Companies around the world continued to deny that CFCs were dangerous. People lost interest, until 1985, when new findings again shocked the world.

Nature's Warning:
The Hole in the Sky

The National Aeronautics and Space Administration (NASA) is the U.S. space agency. It launches satellites into space with all kinds of assignments. One satellite was sent to measure ozone levels in 1978. By the early 1980s, it showed very low ozone amounts above the South Pole. The readings were so low that NASA scientists thought they must be wrong. So the scientists ignored the low readings and said nothing.

British scientists were also measuring ozone at the South Pole. Their project started in 1957. Joseph Farman was the leader of this team. He noticed a drop in ozone every spring beginning in 1977. Farman was puzzled. He could not understand why NASA didn't talk about this problem. Slowly he became sure that there was a hole in the ozone layer. The hole formed each September during the Antarctic spring. It broke up in late October or November.

By 1985, Farman felt he had to speak out. His announcement shocked scientists all over the world. The scientists at NASA went back to check their readings. They found the springtime hole. They also found ozone loss over all of Antarctica. The hole was as deep as Mount Everest is tall. It covered an area as big as the United States. Everyone had known that CFCs could destroy ozone. But until 1985, no one had known how bad the problem was.

Everyone wanted to know more about the hole. Were CFCs responsible? Or could it be due to natural causes, such as a change in radiation from the sun? Was there danger to the ozone layer over the rest of the earth?

22   *Scientists use data collected from ground experiments, air balloon tests, and satellite photos to study the causes and effects of the thinning ozone layer.*

STUDYING THE OZONE HOLE
At the South Pole

Scientists with the National Ozone Expedition went to the South Pole in 1986 and 1987. They used many techniques to study the ozone hole. They used scientific instruments from the ground. They sent giant balloons up to collect data. They also got data from NASA's satellites. Slowly, they put a picture together. They could describe what the sky over the South Pole looked like. But they still did not know for sure what caused the hole.

In August 1987, a new study was begun by top scientists from around the world. The name of this study was the Airborne Antarctic Ozone Experiment. It was based in Chile and was led by NASA.

The scientists used special airplanes loaded with technical instruments. They flew 24 missions during 1988. One plane was a DC-8 that held more than 40 scientists and seven experiments. It flew low so it could look up into the ozone hole.

The scientists also used an ER-2. It is the only plane of its kind in the whole world. It is a modified spy plane— sleek, fast, and small. It held only one pilot and carried scientific instruments under each wing. This plane flew as high as any jet could go. To go higher, you would need a rocket! Flying the ER-2 was dangerous. But it could go right into the ozone hole. And it did—12 times in all.

On September 30, 1988, the first results of the experiment were announced. Scientists now had proof that CFCs caused the hole in the ozone layer. Human-made CFCs were the problem.

Extremely cold temperatures and strong wind storms, combined with the human-made CFCs in the air, create the hole in the ozone layer over the South Pole.

Why Antarctica?

Why was there a hole over the South Pole and nowhere else? Why did it happen in the spring? Scientists kept working until they figured it out.

The South Pole is the coldest place on earth. In the winter, there is no sunlight at all. Powerful winds swirl about the South Pole. The winds whip the air into something called the polar vortex. This swirl of wind does not mix with air from warmer parts of the world. It just gets colder and colder.

The extreme cold makes strange clouds in the Antarctic winter. They form only when the temperature is lower than 112 degrees below zero on the Fahrenheit scale. These cold clouds help to free chlorine. In the spring, the chlorine is free to eat up the ozone. The hole appears. When summer comes, the strange clouds are gone. The winds change. Air filled with ozone rushes in. The hole disappears.

For now, the ozone hole appears only at the South Pole. No place else has exactly this combination of cold and wind. But someday, the same kind of chlorine "Pac-Men" may eat away at ozone all around the world.

HOW BAD IS IT?

The ozone hole over the South Pole may seem far away. But the ozone layer is thinning all around the earth. For the first time, ozone loss is showing up over the North Pole.

NASA brought together another group of more than one hundred scientists to report on global ozone in 1988. Their findings were called the *Ozone Trends Report*. They found that ozone had decreased by as much as 3 percent in the northern half of the world since 1969. This is the half of the world that the United States is in. It also includes Canada, Japan, the Soviet Union, and Europe. The southern half of the world lost even more ozone—up to 5 percent. Ozone loss is happening even faster than computer studies had predicted.

The scientists found that there is another threat to the ozone layer. This is sulfuric acid. These acid droplets are found in the air all over the world. Like the ice crystals at the South Pole, they help CFCs to destroy the ozone.

Ozone loss can be stopped. But it will take a lot of time and work. Even if we stopped making and using products that contain CFCs today, it would take more than one hundred years to stop the loss of ozone. That is because most of the CFCs we have made since 1930 are still rising. They have not yet reached the ozone layer. They will continue to go into the ozone layer for one hundred years.

What will it take to heal the ozone layer? How can we drive CFC levels down below those which caused the hole over the South Pole? A U.S. government agency has some answers. The agency is the Environmental Protection Agency, or EPA. It says

Because of protests like this, many countries are now passing laws to protect the ozone layer.

the world must get rid of all chemicals that destroy ozone. These include CFCs and halons, chemicals used in fire extinguishers. Cleaning solvents also contain some ozone-depleting chemicals. Two of these are methyl chloride and carbon tetrachloride. The EPA also says strict limits must be set for new chemicals used in place of the old ones.

WHAT IS BEING DONE TO SAVE THE OZONE?
A Global Treaty to Protect Ozone

People around the globe face a giant task. We must act to protect and restore the ozone layer. The problem is serious and scary. We have to act quickly! But there is good news. For the first time in history, all countries of the world are working together. And together we can save the ozone layer.

During the summer of 1987, representatives from 43 countries met in Montreal, Canada, to talk about ways to save the ozone layer. After their meeting, they signed the first global treaty on ozone. It is called the Montreal Protocol.

Rich countries make and use more CFCs than poor countries. That is because in rich countries people own more air conditioners and refrigerators. They also buy and use more things made with plastic foam. In other words, they use more CFCs.

Under this treaty, rich countries said they would freeze their production and use of CFCs. They would not make any more CFCs than they did in 1986. And they would start making fewer CFCs each year. By 1999, they promised, they would be making and using only half as many CFCs. Poorer countries, on the other hand, would be permitted to use more CFCs. This would allow them to make necessities like refrigerators for people who had none.

The countries agreed that they could change the treaty if the ozone problem got worse. And the problem did. Just two weeks after the treaty was signed, NASA scientists with the Airborne Experiment reported that CFCs had created the ozone hole. Tougher steps to stop CFCs were needed.

Acting to Save the Ozone

People in countries around the world are putting pressure on lawmakers to protect the ozone layer. They are also putting pressure on companies that make CFCs.

In the United States, five companies make CFCs. Not long ago, they agreed to stop making five of the worst CFCs. Du Pont makes more CFCs than any other company in the world. It has promised to stop by 1999.

These companies are also looking for substitutes for CFCs. Some are already in use. One is Du Pont's HCFC, which is called a "soft" CFC. When a hydrogen (H) molecule is added to the CFC, the compound breaks apart in the lower atmosphere. HCFCs destroy 98 percent less ozone than CFCs do.

Unfortunately, HCFC is a greenhouse gas. Using HCFCs helps to solve one problem—the ozone problem. But it makes worse another problem — global warming. In fact, so far, most of

Scientists are researching new chemicals to do the work done by dangerous CFCs.

the substitutes trade one kind of problem for another. Some add to smog. Some are very expensive to make. Some may cause human health problems. Industries must keep looking for CFC substitutes that are cheap and safe.

A few success stories may encourage them:

• A new solvent to clean electronic parts has been made from orange peels and tree stumps!

• Nissan Motor Company has promised to make an ozone-safe car by 1993. It will stop using CFCs in car seat foam. The biggest problem is finding a substitute to use in car air conditioners.

• General Motors has promised that all its car dealers will recycle the CFCs used in car air conditioners. When cars are serviced, the CFCs will be cleaned and reused. Leaky car air conditioners are the largest source of CFCs in the nation.

• Northern Telecom has said it will stop buying CFCs by the end of 1991. American Telephone and Telegraph Company (AT&T) will stop using CFCs by 1994.

New Laws

Environmental groups are teaching people what they can do to help. Volunteers make phone calls and visit homes. They tell people about the ozone problem. They encourage people to ask for laws to protect the ozone layer.

Many members of the U.S. Congress have ideas for new laws. Some have proposed laws to cut down on the chemicals that destroy ozone. One new law makes U.S. industries report their use of chemicals that destroy ozone. Citizen groups use the informa-

Car exhaust is a major polluter of the atmosphere. By carpooling and taking public transportation, people can reduce the amount of smog in the air.

tion to find out where the ozone-eaters come from. Then they put pressure on the company to make it stop.

That's what citizens did in California, where more damage to the ozone is done than in any other state. In April 1989, more than two thousand people held a protest in San Jose. They marched on International Business Machines (IBM), the number one CFC polluter in California. Citizens help to make changes by putting pressure on polluters.

Some states have also passed laws to cut down on the use of ozone-eaters. Hawaii, Vermont, Oregon, and Connecticut are examples. They were first to pass laws to cut CFC pollution from car air conditioners. Vermont's law will stop all sales of new cars with CFC coolants by 1993. It will not allow the sale of halon fire extinguishers for home use, either. CFC party streamers, noise horns, and dusting sprays will also be banned.

Cities are beginning to make tough new laws, too. They think globally and act locally. They do not wait for the U.S. government to act. Irvine, California, was the first city to act against CFCs. Newark, New Jersey, will ban CFCs in July 1990. Minneapolis and St. Paul, Minnesota, are the third and fourth U.S. cities to propose CFC bans.

The governments of other countries are beginning to act as well. The countries that wrote the Montreal Protocol will sign a new agreement in the future. It will put a faster end to CFC use.

YOU CAN HELP

It will take all of us working together to save the ozone layer. You can do a lot to help.

• Don't buy aerosol cans with CFCs. Spray cans for plastic confetti, like Crazy Strings, contain CFCs. So do cleaning sprays for sewing machines and VCRs. Scientists suggest buying pump sprays instead of aerosols. They do not need gases and are just as easy to use.

• Try not to buy machines or any other items that contain CFCs. Sometimes you can't help it. For example, all refrigerators have CFCs. CFCs are used in making computers. But you can choose to buy many other things without CFCs. Check the label when you buy. Make a list of CFCs on a small card to carry with you. If the product label lists any of these CFCs, buy something else. Here are the CFCs to put on your card:

CFC-11   Trichlorofluoromethane
CFC-12   Dichlorodifluoromethane
CFC-113   Trichlorotrifluoroethane
CFC-114   Dichlorotetrafluoroethane
CFC-115   (Mono) chloropentafluoroethane
Halon-1211   Bromochlorodifluoroethane
Halon-1301   Bromochlorodifluoroethane
Halon-2402   Dibromotetrafluoroethane

• Stay away from polystyrene foam. (This is often called Styrofoam.) This is used for picnic coolers and for foam "pop-

*Non-aerosol containers like these are better for the environment, since they
have no CFCs.*

36

corn" in packages. It is also used to make the foam blocks in shipping boxes. By the end of 1989, most food packages no longer were made with the worst CFCs. But there is no way for consumers to know which types of packages are still made with CFCs. CFCs escape into the air when polystyrene foam is made. They also escape when the foam breaks, crushes, or crumbles. Ask store owners which packages were made with CFCs.

• Do not buy fire extinguishers that contain halon. Even if the fire extinguisher is never used, someday the halons will leak. Then they will rise up into the atmosphere and attack ozone. Instead, buy fire extinguishers that do not use halon.

• Use fans instead of air conditioners. Fans do not use CFCs.

• Does your family car have an air conditioner? If it does, use it less or not at all. If it needs repair, ask your parent to make sure that the repair people recycle CFCs. When it is time to buy a car, choose one that is light-colored and has tinted glass. This will keep the car cooler.

• Watch the packaging that you buy. Many items come in plastics and foams that use CFCs. These create greenhouse gases. They also make lots of trash. Choose products that use less packaging. Look for recycled products. This saves energy, cuts down on waste, and keeps pollution out of the air.

• Watch for CFC-free products. They will be coming out in the next few years. They will be highly advertised. Reward their makers with your business!

• Write to companies that make CFCs. Tell them why you think CFCs are bad. Ask them to stop making CFCs and to find safe substitutes. You can write for the names and addresses of these companies. They are in a free booklet called *Saving the Ozone Layer: A Citizen Action Guide*. The address is on page 40.

• Write to the president and Congress. They make laws that affect your future. They have to decide on laws to ban CFCs and save the ozone. They need to know what all U.S. citizens—even the youngest—think. Writing letters is a way you can help. One letter can change a vote! Sign the letters with your name, address, and age. Find out the names of your senators and representatives, and send your letters to the addresses below:

For your senators:
    The Honorable _____
    United States Senator
    Washington, DC 20510
    Dear Senator _____:

For your representatives:
    The Honorable _____
    U.S. House of Representatives
    Washington, DC 20515
    Dear Representative _____:

For the president:
    President George Bush
    1600 Pennsylvania Avenue NW
    Washington, DC 20500
    Dear President Bush:

Check with your local library for the addresses of your state legislators. Write to them, too!

• Keep informed. Learn the facts. Watch for news of actions that might affect the environment.

• Speak out. Tell others what you have learned. If you convinced two people to do something good for the environment, and the next day they convinced two more people, and so on, it would take less than a month to get everyone in the United States to take action.

FOR MORE INFORMATION

For more information on how you can help save the ozone layer, write to:

The Ecology Center
2530 San Pablo Avenue
Berkeley, CA 94702

Friends of the Earth
218 D Street SE
Washington, DC 20003
  Write for *Atmosphere*, a publication of Friends of the Earth International. It contains the latest news and developments about the ozone layer.

National Wildlife Federation
1400 Sixteenth Street NW
Washington, DC 20036-2266

Natural Resources Defense Council
40 West 20th Street
New York, NY 10011
  Ask for a free copy of *Saving the Ozone Layer: A Citizen Action Guide*.

FOR FURTHER READING

You can learn more about ozone and the environment by reading these books and magazines:

Bach, Julie S., and Lynn Hall, eds. *The Environmental Crisis*. San Diego, Greenhaven Press, 1986.

EarthWorks Group. *50 Simple Things Kids Can Do to Save the Earth*. Berkeley, CA: The EarthWorks Press, 1990.

Gay, Kathlyn. *The Greenhouse Effect*. New York: Franklin Watts, 1986.

————. *Ozone*. New York: Franklin Watts, 1989.

"The Importance of Knowing Sooner." *Odyssey* (January 1989).

Lambert, David. *Planet Earth 2000*. New York: Facts on File, 1985. First published in Great Britain by Purnell Books, Multimedia Publications (UK) Limited, 1985.

Newton, David E. *Taking a Stand Against Environmental Pollution*. New York: Franklin Watts, 1990.

"Our Endangered Planet." *Junior Scholastic* (April 21, 1989).

"Ozone: Saving the Earth's Solar Shield." *3.2.1. Contact* (April 1989).

GLOSSARY

aerosol *A gas that propels another substance; also a container (spray can) that discharges aerosol gases.*

Airborne Antarctic Ozone Experiment *The scientific expedition that discovered the cause of the ozone hole over Antarctica.*

Air Quality Index (AQI) *A scale of numbers used to report on levels of air pollution.*

atmosphere *The blanket of air that surrounds the earth.*

carbon tetrachloride *An ozone-depleting chemical that is used in cleaning solvents.*

cataracts *A clouding of the normally clear and transparent lens of the eye, causing loss of vision and possible blindness.*

chlorine *An ozone-depleting chemical element.*

chlorofluorocarbons (CFCs) *A family of human-made chemicals that are compounds of chlorine, fluorine, and carbon. Used to make foam packaging, coolants, and other products.*

ER-2 *A modified spy plane owned by NASA that can fly to the maximum limits of jet aircraft. Used in the Airborne Experiment to fly into the ozone hole.*

fossil fuels *Energy sources (coal, oil, gas) that formed millions of years ago from the remains of ancient animals or plants. The burning of fossil fuels creates carbon dioxide, a greenhouse gas.*

freon *A CFC gas used in the cooling systems of air conditioners and refrigerators.*

global warming *The belief by some scientists that the earth is slowly warming because of pollutants trapping heat near the earth's surface. Also known as the greenhouse effect.*

greenhouse effect *See* **global warming.** *The belief by some scientists that the earth is gradually warming as a result of a buildup in the atmosphere of heat-trapping carbon dioxide and other gases produced by human activities.*

halon *An ozone-depleting chemical used in fire extinguishers.*

methyl chloride *An ozone-depleting chemical.*

Montreal Protocol *A global treaty signed in 1987 to protect the ozone layer.*

National Ozone Expedition (NOZE) *A study of the ozone over the Antarctic in 1986 (NOZE I) and 1987 (NOZE II).*

oxygen *A gas in the atmosphere. Essential to life.*

ozone *A form of oxygen with three atoms.*

ozone layer *Refers to the protective layer of ozone gas in the stratosphere. It shields the earth from the sun's harmful ultraviolet rays.*

plankton *Microscopic plants and animals in the ocean. Source of food for other ocean creatures.*

Pollutant Standards Index (PSI) *A scale of numbers used to report on levels of air pollution.*

pollutants *Substances that pollute, or contaminate, the environment, such as chemicals, noise, and litter.*

pollution *Anything in the environment that creates unhealthy living conditions.*

polystyrene *Often referred to as Styrofoam. Material used in take-out food containers, egg cartons, and other disposable products.*

recycle (CFCs) *To capture, clean, and reuse CFC gas, particularly in car air conditioners. Recycling helps prevent CFCs from leaking into the atmosphere. It also reduces the need to make new CFCs.*

radiation *Energy transmitted from the sun in the form of waves.*

solvent *Cleaning fluid.*

stratosphere *The zone of the atmosphere from about 8 to 30 miles above the earth's surface.*

troposphere *The part of the earth's atmosphere in which we live. About eight miles thick.*

ultraviolet *An invisible part of the sun's radiation (light energy) that is harmful to life.*

ultraviolet-B *A form of ultraviolet radiation that can cause skin cancer.*

INDEX